Table of Cc

CW00546690

About King Carl Mensah

My name is Carl Mensah known as King Carl Mensah and I am 26 years old from Croydon. I grew up in Denmark Hill, near Camberwell in South East London and I'm from Ghana and Nigeria, as you can see from my last name. I am a boxer, a motivational speaker, entrepreneur and author.

The reason why I do what I do is because I believe in empowering people towards greatness to become the best version of themselves. I believe that if people use their gifts and talents in the right way, the world will be a better place.

This smile shows the comeback in on!!!

The Best Comeback King in the World

The Best Comeback King in the World..... The Best Comeback King in the World..... The Best Comeback King in the World.... What was King Carl coming back from?

- What adversities did I have to overcome?

I was a kid who had no confidence. I struggled with finding my identity. I was a victim of bullying in school and I've had my phone robbed which was a big part of my story.

Now I have confidence, I know who I am and I'm now a boxer, a motivational speaker, an entrepreneur and author.

- How did I make a comeback? How did I find myself? How did this all start for me?

I found my gifts and talents at 16 and went through the process of unlocking the greatness within myself.

- How did you do it King Carl?

- This book is for two sets of people, the first is the person who may be asking: "Why am I in this world?"

- You may be in transition, and you may be thinking where do I go from here?

- What's next for me?

- What value do I bring to this world?

Also, this book is for anyone who wants to elevate their lives to become the best version of themselves no matter how much success they have currently. I believe there are always ways that we can improve to become the Kings and Queens we are destined to be.

If you see yourself as a champion, a King, a Queen, a conqueror, a warrior, a winner, an entrepreneur, a leader, a visionary, a parent looking to empower your children/teenagers or a creative person looking to make the world a better place. If your answer is yes to any of these questions, then this book is for you.

I'm passionate about people becoming the best version of themselves and using their gifts and talents to change the world. I believe there are some things about ourselves that make us unique and great that separates us from other people. Throughout this book I will be sharing my process and what I've overcome to be the best comeback king in the world and how you can be the best comeback king or queen in the world.

You may not have had someone in your life that can see the greatness in you and even though we may have not met before, I see greatness in you.

Let's tune out the noise on the outside and tune into your greatness on the inside.

CHAPTER 1
Destruction

This picture below shows a quick glimmer of the comeback king story near the end, loool, keep reading on for more...

I went to English Martyns primary school which was near East Street market. I used to get into many fights with a few people from my class. It was time and time again that I would get into trouble. I would always be outside the head teacher's office. My parents had to be called. I remember coming home one time and my dad say it was fine or sometimes I would lie and say that Maths and English was good. Then, he would say .... "Mrs Appah called me" and I

would know in my head that he knew about the fight I'd had that day. My dad would always emphasize the same thing "tell the teacher "If someone was annoying me, but I never listened. I always used to get grounded. If you are coming from an African background like me, you can relate to the struggle; especially if you got in trouble!

There was a time where my dad would come to the school and sit inside the classroom. I hated it! It felt awkward; but he was there to make sure that my behavior was under control. I knew it must have been very hard for my mum and dad to teach me the right ways however, I was involved in many fights. I remember once when my dad drove myself and my two sisters to Mauldsey Hospital. My Dad, said that this man, who was walking towards us, was going to take me away. I was young and I was really fearful, as he opened the door, thinking that the man was going to take me to the hospital and take me away. Of course, that's not what happened, it was a trick; my dad's way of trying to stop me fighting and getting into trouble in school.

This is how it felt in primary school. I was always getting into fights and people used to annoy me all the time.

I remember a time when I was accused of bullying a girl in my class in primary school. They thought that I was copying her to take the mick out of her because of her accent. In all honesty, I was but I didn't know it was classified as bullying. I was around people that were doing the same thing, so I just copied them. It just shows, the first rule to learn is to get around the right people, otherwise you will always be in trouble.

I had a conversation with my mum and she told me when I was in primary school, I didn't really respect female teachers. This was a very interesting realization, because that was true, only if the teacher was not too nice because this approach for building me up into a man doesn't work from my perspective. As I progressed during the years in secondary school the female teachers were firm with me and didn't take any nonsense from anyone. My mum is a firm, fair, loving and caring woman, however I needed a different voice on a male's side which I got from my dad, as I briefly explained above. Also, I needed other male role models that were not my parents that could help me on my journey from a boy to a man. I'm sure you have heard the saying "it takes a village to raise a child," this is very true.

On the other hand, I have to say, I did have a great teacher in year 4 who was a very disciplined teacher that was able to speak through to me if I was in trouble, as he spoke through to me with wise words. He was a great male role model in my school to look up to, as we could relate. He always wanted to make sure that we became a better version of ourselves if we were going off track. I believe this is what would have helped me more if I had a mentor consistently throughout my time in primary school that could guide me through my anger management challenges.

KING CARL'S I AM A KING MINDSET TIPS

King Carl's boxing ready – an outlet that's helped me with anger management and having a mental release

I believe that having a great male role model especially as a boy is something that I advise for every boy to have. You become what you think about and what you see. So, if you see someone that's guiding you in the right direction it will be better for you in the short and long term which is what helped me.

On the other hand, something that I believe helped me to manage anger and gave me an outlet for stress, depression and anxiety, was boxing. I believe that it gave me a great outlet for my mind, fitness, self-discipline and self-control, which we all need. There have been many benefits for me, including helping to boost my self-confidence. Also, learning a combat sport such as boxing, helps you to know how to defend and protect yourself and others.

In addition, one of the big reasons why I got into boxing was because I've had my phone robbed. At the time it happen, it made me very fearful and cautious. I'm not going to go too much into it, but this is one my biggest motivations, because I never want to be in a position again where I feel hopeless, or my self-confidence has been taken away. One of my secrets is that I use what happen to me to my advantage, as a powerful motivational tool to conquer and win which is what happened when I had to comeback and win my first boxing match.

I'm still in the early stages of my boxing journey and I've already seen and felt these benefits for me personally, so I encourage anyone to do it even just as a fitness outlet and you will see the benefits that I'm talking about. I also believe it helps with creativity of business ideas because your mind is clearer due to the intense activities that boxing requires to empower yourself to become the best version of yourself.

KING CARL'S EMOTIONALMANAGEMENT JOURNAL

I have a question for you....

- How do you manage your emotions and anger?

  _____

  _____

  _____

  _____

  _____

- What are your outlets that helps you with pressure, stress, anger, anxiety, fear and any other emotion that may be a burden to you?

  _____

  _____

  _____

  _____

  _____

If you are a person that struggles with anger management like I did and you want more ways that helped me and that is still helping me today.

Connect with me further on social media to carry on the conversation through my social media Instagram, TikTok, LinkedIn Facebook and, Twitter @kingcarlmensah

I AM KING MINDSET FRAMEWORK TIP

REMEMBER THE I AM A KING MINDSET

K – Knowledge

I – Inspire

N – Not caring about what other people think

G – Goals

Watch my next process into secondary school; it was a tough and interesting time. From fighting in school to being bullied. How? Keep reading to find out more....

CHAPTER 2
On the way down

The transition to St Joseph's College an all-boys school, which I didn't want to go to, was different because I wanted to go to Sacred Heart in Camberwell, a mixed school. It was a jump into the unknown which was a scary thing for me. I remember one of the first days of me starting at St Joseph's College, I didn't want my mum to drop me off in front of the school, because I would have felt embarrassed if she did. Year 7 was a huge jump from year 6 where you think you're on top of the world because you are in primary school.

The jump from primary to secondary school was a huge difference. I had to grow up quickly, just like I was confident in taking this picture a long time ago loool, anyways back to the story

Secondary school was... interesting. I came into year 7 with a bag that was bigger than me! It's funny looking back on it now. My time in an all- boys school was hectic and a thrilling ride of ups and downs. I was the quiet kid in year 7, as I used to get bullied. I lacked confidence in myself and had low self-esteem.

This may confuse you; how do I start getting bullied after I always used to get into fights myself? It just made me think did my primary school days soften me, or was it preparing for me the war that was ahead of me? However, it was annoying to me because people were taking the mick out of me such as calling me a "T- REX," Saying that I was dead at football and more stuff that always used to get into my head and I started to believe the lies that I was told. When you have people saying negative things about you that's not true it can get into your head, especially in secondary school.

I believe that secondary school was survival of the fittest.

As this was going on it affected me mentally, as I didn't even want to play football for PE which was a sport that I loved. However, due to the negative comments people were saying about me, it put me off the sport at the time. The negative words that people used to say to me really affected me and I was also cautious of who I was around because I knew they wanted to pick on me like I was a victim.

My point is that anyone that is going through this is that there is light at the end of the tunnel and keep reading on to find my ways of my comeback.

Also, ATTENTION to all the BULLIES and people saying negative things about people YOU NEED TO STOP doing it because you can re ally take someone down into a dark place and make them fearful and always on edge because they think something bad is going to happen.

Bullying in person or online needs to STOP NOW. BULLYING IS STILL BULLYING. DON'T BE A COWARD AND MOVE AWAY FROM THAT STUFF because it doesn't lead to anything good. You can also, follow my journey and take this energy and transfer it into something positive instead of using it on someone else that you think your better than. Trust me, when you meet your match, you would not like it. I've seen and heard of these stories many times before and it doesn't end good!

There used to be this boy in school that always used to put me into headlocks and it was very annoying. He used to keep doing it and it used to frustrate me, so much to my breaking point. I remember there was a time where I said to myself if he touches me again, "I don't care if his back breaks". It was a harsh statement, but a very true one for me because I was very angry and I felt caged in. I didn't feel that telling the teacher will do anything because in school people used to call it snitching. I needed to fight back, but I wasn't strong enough and I didn't have the muscle. I had my friends trying to back me up, but how long is that going to last for? There used to be other people who used to pick on

At this time of my life as a youth, I didn't call myself King Carl, it was more like I'm lost, I'm confused, I have a low self-image and I was low in confidence. I wasn't the only one, as there were other people who were bullied as well. I couldn't defend myself, let alone others.

I used to go to class early and stand outside my tutor's classroom, just because I was too afraid to talk to girls.

When it came to PE time, I had mixed emotions. The reason was because I was always one of the last to be picked in school when it came to football and other sports that we did. I always got told to go into defense because people said I was not good enough, so that affected me, every time I tried to grow with confidence someone came to shut it down.

I had a negative belief system about myself that I was fat, slow and even I used to get called a T-Rex which didn't help my process to become more confident in myself. There was a time when we were playing football and I thought I was going to pass the ball to my teammate and I kicked the grass and fell on the floor. Everyone was laughing at me, and my confidence went out of the window yet again. I was trying to smile and act like everything was ok but, it wasn't. I really thought I was going to pass the ball like Xavi when he was playing at Barcelona but, this didn't happen. It just felt like my self-belief was being chipped away, day by day. It was just always doom and gloom for me.

I was very insecure about my weight and what people thought about me because I was chubby. When it came to swimming, this was another challenge that I had to overcome because I was fearful that people would call me fat. Maybe this is you that's reading this? Maybe you can also relate to the struggle? You're not on your own. In addition, to this since I'm talking about confidence and sports, I have another story where it comes to cross country, do you remember that? I used to get so tired and I was nowhere near the finish line, I would be one of the last ones to finish and my self-image was low as well.

There were more interesting experiences when it came to my time at SJC as time progressed. I used to see people selling kit-kats, doughnuts, gold bars and breakaways to make some money which I understood at the time. I'll share with you my story as my mum used to make me nice sandwiches for packed lunch. I had someone from my English class who wanted to buy hula hoops from me. I didn't want to sell the hula hoops, so I opened the packet, poured some in his hand and said it's one pound and he paid and I had the rest. I believe that's probably where my stubbornness in business came from.

Time was passing by during secondary school and more progression was being made, as I was getting older-- my confidence in myself started to grow and I started to stand up for myself more. When it was home time at SJC, most of the times it was every Friday that we went on the 68 bus and we did royal rumble just like in WWE, even when they told us not to try it at home. I was still quiet at the time, however there was a youth that was a year below me, trash talking to me, so we resolved it at the back of the bus, and we fought. I stood up for myself and held my ground. I don't encourage you fighting on the bus, but I'm just sharing with you my journey of how I became who I am today.

I believe that standing up for yourself is an important factor for me that helped increase my confidence. I felt more uplifted and the it seemed the rise of a King was going to be known. I will also explain a bit about the King Carls' turning point in the next chapter.

The process at SJC goes on... Being from another school, if another school wants to start trouble, they will also find an excuse to do so. I remember the people I was going home with; we came off the 468 bus and we were waiting for the 68 and kids from another school was making threats. Like I said to you before, some people just wanted to start something for absolutely no reason, which is pointless.

A warrior mentality was needed in school. It was survival of the fittest.

> I REMEMBER A MEMORY WHEN I WON MY FIRST TAEWON-DO COMPETITION, THIS WAS THE MINDSET NEEDED TO SURIVIVE IN SCHOOL.

A winning mentality.

I cannot, go on without sharing you my experience, when my face nearly got lit up with a firework. I was standing near the door of the chicken shop and I believe it was bomb fire night and there were youths across the road and they aimed to throw it inside the chicken shop, which they did, but it skinned my face. I'm too pretty for all of that for my face to get lit up! It was like living on edge when you were at SJC. I remember seeing a knife in school, there was a lot going on. It's like everyone was trying to find themselves and fit in.

My extra skills that were developed helped me become the person that I am today. I don't care what anyone says to you, your life is not finished, there is greatness in you. If it can happen for me, it can happen for you.

I have more information that goes over more on how to gain confidence within yourself.

This is how you will feel and look at the end of your come-back in your storm of life

KING CARL'S - I AM A KING MINDSET TIP

I believe one of the practices that helped me develop the I AM A KING MINDSET, was the affirmations that I say to myself which I can show you.

For example, declare that that you are a King or Queen destined for greatness. I AM A KING, I AM A QUEEN, I AM A CHAMPION, I AM A WINNER, I AM WARRIOR, I OVERCOME ANY CHALLENGES THAT COME MY WAY IN LIFE!!!

I believe that when you affirm your greatness to yourself it increases your belief system in YOU.

KING CARL'S I AM A KING GROWTH BUILDER ACTIVITY

- What are the ways that you build your self confidence in your-self?

  _____
  _____
  _____
  _____
  _____

- What ways do you think you can increase your self-confidence TODAY?

  _____
  _____
  _____
  _____
  _____

My overall summary of my time in secondary school was hectic, interesting and challenging. I know what happens in school, especially as I have been through it. I believe in empowering the youth and adults towards greatness because there is a powerful story in you that the world needs to hear.

Tag me on my social media and share what you have learnt with me on @kingcarlmensah

Instagram, Tiktok, Facebook, LinkedIn, Twitter

CHAPTER 3
The Turning point

Fitting in

I remember whiles I was at Christ the King 6th Form College, I wanted to fit in because I felt insecure and out of place. I had Primark plimsoles and I saw everyone else in college with Prada, Gucci and all the high- end designer brands. It seemed like a place where everyone was following the famous crowd and people wanted to impress others, especially as there were girls there. I remember going out with my older sister, to get some new trainers, air forces to be exact. I was adamant to have some new trainers to fit into the crowd. I remember my sister said that the air forces were too big for me, as I got a size 9 when I should have got a size 8, but they didn't have it in stock.

However, I still said I wanted the trainers. When I got home, I realized they were big because when I tried them on again, I can only wear three pairs of thick socks to put them on. Then, it came to the time when I went to college and it was the most embarrassing moment ever that I didn't want to experience again. You know there's that one person that is so nosy and always in your business? That person decided to pree my trainers and say "I swear they're big for you." I didn't know what to do at this point. This was all because I wanted to fit in and be like everyone else. I was insecure in myself and who I was. Can you relate? Why did I want to fit into the crowd so much, not knowing that I was born to stand out?

The girl that played me

Why fit in, when your chosen by God? You have greatness in YOU

I remember thinking that this girl that I saw in college was feeling me and then I realized she played me the whole time... I had warning signs from my friends who I was chilling with, and they said she's playing you Carl but, I didn't listen because I thought that they were jealous. There was a time where I thought she liked me because she hooked her arm under my arm thinking that she was my girl, so I was gassed up! When really, I was just a sideman for her and her friends. But you know why this happened? I was trying to impress girls and fit in, instead of taking time to find out who I am. The story is not finished, so as I continue when it came to the last day of college, I was gassed and I was speaking to everyone even if I didn't talk to them all year. It was the last day of college and I saw her on the bus, so I sat next to her and said will you miss me, and she looked at me, smirked and said no and she came off the bus. At that moment I was hurt and shocked. That was where my guard went up and I thought to myself why do I keep doing this thing to myself where I'm trying to impress others? Seeking validation is not the way forward, we need to find ourselves and what makes us the best.

That's how I was feeling, at first when I asked her, will she miss me but, that wasn't the mood at the end looool

King Carl's trend setting

I believe that this was my story of being a trend setter and one of the moments where I took a stand of who I was and creating my own path.

One of the reasons why I went to the library so much was because I didn't really have a lot of friends when I was at Christ the King. I had people who were in my class and in other classes and people that I knew who had a friendship through others but, apart from that I didn't really have a lot of people. This is where I started to feel out of place and lonely, so I went to the library and I went to do self-development and listen to audios and work on myself. I remember most times when I went to the library I was taken the mick out of, and I was called a neek from some people I was hanging around with. Then one day I said I'm going to zone out and work on myself and then there was a time when I said I'm going to the library, this time the person that was with me said "I might as well go too," so then I realized for myself I was becoming a trend setter. I remember there were many times people started to come to the LRC as well to do work like me. I even had someone in my class see me listening to self-development audios to improve myself and they were inspired.

When you start creating your own lane and being you, you begin to attract opportunities to become a better version of yourself. This was me speaking in Croydon and winning one of the toastmaster's prizes, empowering the people with my speech.

I was in my zone. I also remember there was a time where I was improving so much that another student who was a business minded person, collaborated with me to create ideas for the next big thing. We went off to an office place in the college next to the careers department. We were mapping out different ideas that we could create and make money. We were just hustling, and we wanted to win in life. This was where some of my entrepreneurship and business journey started, and it was also where I didn't believe in restrictions and being boxed in a cage. Even during my time where I was very business minded my form tutor, knew that I was destined for greatness because of my determination to win and get better.

Winning the Toastmasters Speakers of Croydon award

More speaking opportunities as King Carl's journey expands

King Carl's Major Change

This was my time when I was 16 years old working at Sports Direct. My manager said "snake the tables" which means fix the boxes. I took that as he was talking down to instead of speaking to me as a human. This is properly where I got my motivation to not be restricted from and be capped from anything and anyone. At that moment I remember when I said to God, "you need to sort him out before I sort him out". I didn't fight him or anything but, that was the moment for me where things had to change. I remember reading a scripture that says "A man's gift will make room before great men." Proverbs 18 -16 which was what helped me find who I am today. I was searching for what I was gifted and talented at. I wrote down on a piece of paper anything that I thought I was good at, or I wanted to do. The first thing I wrote down was coaching. I wrote down other things such as motivational speaking, my own business, be a comedian and more. I remember going back to the club I used to play for which was Greenhouse FC and I went to the club, and I said to the coach I'm only here to see if coaching was something I needed to do. I didn't care about any contract; I was seeking for why I was here. I remember the first time I was coaching the kids who were about 4-6 years old, I felt I was baby-sitting them and not coaching. However, I remember saying to myself I'm going to be there long enough where I know if I need to be doing coaching or not. The turning point for me was when I was coaching the kids and my session overran, then I knew at that moment I was supposed to use my gift of speaking and empowering people especially the youth.

> **"Travel because, money returns, time doesn't."**

The reason why I knew so clearly that I needed to do this was because I was very passionate about it. At the end of this session, I remember saying to one of the coaches I was with, I want to go abroad. Then after that I found out that one of the coaches went off to USA and I wanted to go there as well. I didn't have the money to go there at the time I decided to go, however I was very determined that nothing could stop me. The contract landed on my birthday June 2nd. This was my birthday present for me to be honest. I found out that I was flourishing as a coach, to uplift people towards greatness to became the best version of themselves.

I believe the reason I found that scripture was because I wanted to find out why I was in the world and what was my purpose in life. The time period at sports direct was making me realize that while I was doing this job just for money, it also gave me a sense of urgency to find out why I was here and to also know what my passion was. One of the main factors that helped me find out my gift was not just the scripture but, also listening to Steve Harvey who is a great comedian and very motivational and he said "Your gift is the thing that you do with the least amount of effort." When he said this, it hit me because, as I was in the process of seeking what this was, I found out one of my gifts is speaking and uplifting people at any given time with my words. I believe it was empowering when I encountered Steve Harvey because it gave me a different perspective while I was searching for my gifts.

During my process of being me, there was more discoveries along the way, such as boxing for me which is currently something I'm a part of right now.

King Carl's boxing journey expanded to the USA (Houston)

KING CARL'S I AM A KING MINDSET TIP

One tip that I would give that's helped me, has been the power of visualization and the power to create a vison board that can help you think big and that anything is possible. This is a group of pictures of what you want to have and it is glued on a piece of paper. This has helped keep my mind focused when other distractions come in my way.

SEE YOURSELF HIGHER, SEE YOURSELF AS A KING, SEE YOURSELF AS A QUEEN THAT'S GOING TO CHANGE THE WORLD FOR BETTER!!!

KING CARL – I AM A KING AND I AM A QUEEN MINDSET ACTIVITY

- Where do you see yourself in the next year?

  _____

  _____

  _____

  _____

  _____

- What do want to accomplish within the next year?

  _____

  _____

  _____

  _____

  _____

- Where do you see yourself in 5 years?

  _____

  _____

  _____

_____

_____

- What will you be doing if you had all the money and time in the world?

_____

_____

_____

_____

_____

CHAPTER 4
The Comeback

My transition from Christ the King to Westminster Kingsway College which was a big jump into something different because it was an entrepreneurship academy called the Peter Jones Academy. I wanted to do an apprenticeship because I knew I was a practical person. Then I was led to this course for a year, which I liked the sound of, so I went for it and did it. I believe that one of the first things that we must do is take risks even though it may be scary and uncomfortable, but this is the only way that we grow.

When you connect with greatness, you believe more is possible. Great connecting with Mr Des O'Connor

Business networking events to connect with the right people to grow more into the KING I AM

*Great to connect with Balbir who is a very well-connected business man and also a vibrant **person** as you can see in the picture below.*

The Peter Jones Academy was a real entrepreneurship academy for me where I felt that you were given the space to flourish and develop who you were, especially in the business area. There was creativity that was birthed inside me. We had opportunities to do practical work but, also, we had to do coursework at times which was boring but, we learned to persevere and move forward even if not all the modules were fun.

There were different experiences that helped me to grow as a person and develop a love for exploring, which were my trips to

South Korea and Portugal. The interesting thing about my trip to South Korea is that my teacher Mrs Irene offered the trip to me for free, but however I rejected it initially because I was scared. It was strange for me.

Especially, travelling for 13 hours. I nearly allowed FEAR to cost me enjoying my experience. The reason I went was because I had a friend in college named Nathan, who went so I went with the other people who were in my college but, they were not on my course. When I went to South Korea, I believe it was one of the best travel experiences that I've had because I took a jump into the unknown and the people there were nice and friendly. I was there for two months on an exchange program where I was teaching English and then I was learning the Korean language and the culture. This was an adventure that helped me grow into the person that I am today.

I encourage anyone to go on a traveling adventure just like I did it will really expand your mind. This was a hands-on practical course that allowed me to develop myself as an entrepreneur.

> **This was one of King Carl's business adventures in the USA exploring**

In addition, to this at the end of the time at Westminster Kingsway College, I had a trip to Portugal with people from my class as it was an end of year trip to explore and go on another adventure. This was a funny experience because there was a lot of vibes and energy in the city. I remember there were times when we went to a party festival and it was LIVE!!! We went to go and explore the city and the food, everyone had fun; it was a time to remember.

During my time at WKC, I was in the enterprise society group where we came up with different ideas to help improve the college, the course, raising money through charity and fund-raising events that we hosted. I remember there was a time where we hosted a cooking show where Levi Roots who is well known for reggae sauce was also there. Adding to this we had a fashion show where there were different people modeling on stage, I was one of them of course! It was my time to shine, loool!!! We as a group thought of collective ways to be creative and to think of something out of nothing.

Are you struggling with the process of finding yourself and using the creativity within yourself that you don't even know? Are you in a transition and you don't know what is next for your life? Do you feel that you don't know what's going to happen next, don't worry I've been there.

I received a certificate in South Korea for my global exchange program that I took part in. I learnt Korean and taught English to children.

KING CARL'S I AM A KING - CREATIVE CHALLENGE

- What do you believe that you are gifted at or you do naturally without even knowing?

_____

_____

_____

_____

_____

- What are you passionate about?

_____

_____

_____

_____

Tag me on social media and hashtag #passion and let me know what your passionate about.

@kingcarlmensah on all social media platforms

CHAPTER 5
The Unknown

UCFB Wembley (University Campus of Football Business) was my university that I went to and it was a massive shock in my journey-- I didn't want to go in the first place. I wanted to do an apprenticeship because I knew I was a practical and hands on person. This was the jump I took from WKC and South Korea into university. I remember when I was in South Korea and I was lying down on my bed and I was thinking to myself what am I going to do when I get back to the UK. I went on google and wrote different topics such as football, business, enterprise and entrepreneurship. I remember also calling my parents while I was in South Korea and telling them that I was going to university to do this course. Then I remember a course that popped up which was called Football Business and Marketing and I realized that UCFB was a university. I then made up in my mind that I will go to UCFB because I liked the look of the university which was different, and I liked football.

Another reason was because I had experience in marketing. I chose the course for the wrong reasons I believe, which I will explain a bit more in my content at the end of this chapter if you want to find out more.

So now I've managed to get the role at UCFB which was through clearance. I went to see the university and I liked the set up and the vibes within the area. The tour that I went on with my mum in Wembley stadium was great because I remember going to the England changing room and going outside in Wembley stadium. The environment was built up for success and it was a great way to explore and expand my mind due to the awareness on the field.

Great to meet the Arsenal legend, Patrick Vieira. I'm an Arsenal fan too!!!

During my time at UCFB I will be honest, the first time I was there it was great, and it was a nice feel. I liked the environment, the set up and the people. However, as I progressed through the course especially at the start of the year, I started to realize that I had chosen this course out of convenience and for the guaranteed job, that I thought having the knowledge of marketing would give me when I finished. But I was not using the gifts and talents that I knew I had, which was to empower people and coach others to help them be the best version of themselves. I was consumed by fear and caught up with mentally following what the world dictated. I picked marketing because the sector is vast and because it was more likely to get me a job. I later discovered there was a course called Football Coaching and Management which was more of what I wanted to do. I knew in my heart I could do this role at the university and that my gifts would flourish and make room for me to be more of who I am.

I wanted to quit within the first year. I remember when I was coming in the morning to Wembley Stadium for 9am lectures and after I had to work at Adidas normally around 4pm after university finished until roughly 10pm. This is retail, so you don't finish on time and then from there I had to take a train home for about 1hr 30 – 2hrs most times during the week that I was in uni. When I got home at roughly 12am I was considering, do I eat, or do I go to bed because I had to wake up early in the morning and leave around 7- 7.30am in the morning to be on time to the lecture. There were many times where I was late and, I would skip lectures and seminars which I wouldn't advise. There were times where I would go to another course and go and be with the football manager of the university, named Jay and I would be with him while he was coaching the first team in football. I remember there were many times I would go and see the teams play and I was so determined to learn, it would be icy on the field and my feet and hands were cold but, I wanted to be a coach. There will also be times I would get the opportunity to give advice for the team which was great for me. I would go and look for extra courses that I could do to increase my knowledge in football and how to coach even though this was not my course. I was passionate about empowering people and coaching because it was one of the gifts that I was given to offer this world and make this world better.

After having these feelings of wanting to quit, I pushed through because it was too late to go onto another course within the first year. I then had to persist and be resilient in something that I wanted to shift away from.

Due to my persistence, I pushed through and I managed to get a 3rd. For me this was like a, 1st as I was dancing on stage even though I was told not to. It was vibes all day and shout out to my older sister for helping me push through. Shout out to Lipa also, if you're reading this.

Remember, the vibes on the stage, loool, we took over!

KING CARL'S I AM A KING TIP

Something that helped me during my process at uni, when I was in a transition was that I was always networking with new people that help me grow. There is a famous saying, called, "your network is your net worth," so I would advise get involved in any other community programs, such as community outreach, student union, football coaching in the area or anything that may interest you. Ask how you can get involved and serve and add value. I remember I was doing this with Jay the Football Manager, as I briefly explained before.

> "Grow your mind, grow your life, and grow your network champions"!

KING CARL'S QUOTE

KING CARL'S I AM A KING MINDSET ACTIVITY

- What do you do when you are unsure what to do in life?

  _____

  _____

  _____

  _____

  _____

- I have a question for the students who are currently in university right now... Do you have an expectation for when you finish uni?

  _____

  _____

  _____

  _____

  _____

- Have you already finished uni and are not in the place you thought you would be?

  _____

  _____

  _____

  _____

  _____

- Do you see the future for you, after uni?

  _____

  _____

  _____

  _____

  _____

- Do you feel lost within your journey?

  _____

  _____

  _____

  _____

  _____

- Are you in a place where you believe you have made a wrong decision, or you have made a wrong turn in life?

  _____

  _____

  _____

  _____

  _____

I've been there before, and I understand the process.

Connect with me on social media. if you don't have me already and #uni chapter so we can speak more. I'm here to serve you so that you can be the King or Queen that your destined to be in life.

Tag me and say what you took from this chapter.

My social media handles are @kingcarlmensah on Instagram, Tik-Tok, LinkedIn, Facebook and Twitter.

CHAPTER 6
Ultimate Guidance

I believe that during my transition there was a huge amount of uncertainty. When I was on the hunt to find out who I am and finding what my gifts and talents are, it was tough for my parents from their perspective. I was in my transition from when I was 16, trying to find out who I was and why I was in the world. What's my purpose in life? I was really on a mission to find out why I was here, what made me tick? What were my gifts and talents? However, during this transition it was challenging for my parents because they heard me say one thing and then I was doing another. I remember there was a time where my dad came to check on me in my room and I was confused with myself because I didn't know where I was going, I couldn't give a clear direction. I didn't believe in being boxed in cages of limitations and things that I was not called to do, when I knew deep down in my heart I was destined for more.

This was one of motivational mantras on Monday that I created to empower people to become the best version of themselves.

This was a challenge through the big changes that I was making from sports direct, to coaching and businesses that I was running as well. I would say one thing that my parents never did, is that they didn't force me to do anything. Since I was on the hunt for finding out what my gifts and talents were, when I knew coaching was what I wanted to do, they didn't stop me, even though they did not know everything about what I was doing.

My parents advised me the best way that they could as parents would. However, I had the mindset that I believe in creating and I don't believe jobs, or anything is guaranteed unless we guarantee ourselves. I believe in creating something out of nothing. So, as you can see there were conflicting beliefs.

KING CARL'S TIP

I believe that one way that helped me during my process of connecting with young people, as a youth leader, mentor and sports coach was realising that young people want to be heard and listened to. They want to know that their voice matters and that they are cared for. I also believe that being able to relate to them and understand them, is a key factor, that I have realised helps in the process of empowering them to become the Kings and Queens that they are destined to be.

- This area is a huge topic and I have much more to share with you, on the other hand I wanted to ask a few questions?

_____

_____

_____

_____

_____

KING CARL'S ACTIVITY FOR PARENTS WITH CHILDREN/ TEENAGERS

- What are the ways that you connect with your children/ teenager to understand them more?

  _____

  _____

  _____

  _____

  _____

- What are some of the challenges that you may be having with your child or teenager at this moment?

  _____

  _____

  _____

  _____

  _____

- Do you feel disconnected from your child / teenager or young adult?

  _____

  _____

  _____

  _____

  _____

- Do you find that your child/teenager/young adult doesn't want to speak to you or open up?

  _____

  _____

_____

_____

_____

Tag me on social media and share with me anything that may been of value for you in this section. Also, message me on my social media below to see how I could be of service to you on @kingcarlmensah My LinkedIn, Facebook, Instagram, Twitter and Tiktok

The Kingdom Review

I believe that the transition for me out of uni was where I decided even more to make sure that I worked on my gifts and talents more in my life. What I did after university was work on my gift that I was given which was empowering others. What I did was to make sure that I searched out roles in schools, coaching and uplifting the youth. I would take teaching assistant roles at schools through agencies because I wanted to uplift the youth and instill confidence in them. During this time, I also had a business as well which I was working on because I believed in entrepreneurship.

This is myself, with professional boxing champion Joshua Buatsi, who was from Croydon boxing academy, which is where I train. He is known as the former British and, WBA Intercontinental Light Heavyweight champion and Olympic Bronze medallist. He is also from Ghana and is from Croydon.

Exploring our creativity wasn't something encouraged in school and also networking with others. Getting out of your comfort zone and meeting the right people.

I met Mr Spencer Fearson who's well known in the boxing era. We met at a business event I got connected through Mr Des O'Connor

I remember there were times during my journey where I would have moments where I needed to change. I remember there was a moment where I was on a business call and then I got off the call and I was told, "do it." I was procrastinating on the fact that I was not working on my motivational speeches. I remember straight after that call that I had, I started to speak on my Instagram. Can you imagine I said things that were wrong? However, the fact that the video was not perfect but, it was authentic and real which is what connected with people. The overall summary of the message was to start now and stop procrastinating which was what was holding me back.

During this time of my transition, I was really on a mission to coach more, so I was taking my FA Level 2 coaching badge and, I was doing Futsal, as well because I was passionate about empowering the youth. I would want to improve myself and get better all the time. This transition was really to explore more of who I was, as time went on. I was discovering more about myself as I grew into more of who I was, which is where my confidence grew even more within myself.

Transitions are scary and not comfortable places especially when you have not experienced it before because nothing is guaranteed. However, transitions in our lives are needed for us to grow into who we are.

I was told many times that I wasn't good enough, especially during my time in school. This affected me, but look where I am now! I am a KING and a WINNER. The reason why I wrote this book is to share with people that it doesn't matter what your circumstances are or where you have started in life, you can still be the best comeback king or queen in the world.

Man like Mighty Myke – great to meet with energy
and greatness

One thing that I realized about myself is that you can't put me in a box of limitations because I don't stay there. I am a creative king destined for greatness and you are destined for greatness too.

> **I'm now a boxer, a motivational speaker, an entrepreneur and an author.**

This is one of my Coaches at Croydon Boxing Academy, co the owner. Mr Shane Sobers. He has helped me massively on this journey and still continues to do so as we keep moving.

When you discover who you are and find what you are destined to do, you find life. Proverbs 18 -16 was the scripture that changed my life and helped me on my process of life "a man's gift will make room, before great men."

REMEMBER THE I AM A KING MINDSET

K – Knowledge

I – Inspire

N – Not caring about what other people think

G – Goals

Connect with me more on social media for more of the break-downs of the I AM A KING MINDSET.

Strive and prosper to the top where you belong! And remember to rise and shine and have fun.

Blessings all and remember you are GREAT and UNIQUE. The world needs YOU so be YOU and do YOU.

Follow me on all of my socials

Instagram - @kingcarlmensah TikTok - @kingcarlmensah Linkdin - @kingcarlmensah Facebook - @kingcarlmensah Twitter - @king-carlmensah

Youtube - @kingcarlmensahofficial

Sponsors- AssureTax Accountants

I have to say a huge thank you to my first sponsor Assure Tax Accountants for helping me get my book over the line to reach the masses today. Mr Jayen C Patel, I really appreciate this, as it was great to have a local sponsor based in Croydon that saw my vision that I was sharing on my book, to empower people to become the best version of themselves. I again really appreciate this help, to turn a dream to reality and to now share my story globally around the world.

What Director, of AssureTax Accountants had to say:

"Carl since reading your story I was instantly captivated with some of the similarities in my own life journey as well as others I know. The life experiences you have encountered and how you have turned this around through the use of sport & fitness, personal development and your positive bright mindset, to emerge as you are today, will bring true hope and inspiration to many reading your book. Your footprint will be felt and embraced to bring light to so many others also experiencing their own life challenges today.
Keep treading with this mission Carl. It's your purpose. Well done!!!

Director of AssureTax Accountants – Mr Jayen C Patel

This is me with Director, Mr Jayen C Patel

For any great accountancy services, please contact AssureTax Accountants below:

Telephone number – 0208 666 0223

Website - www.assuretax.co.uk

Contact Mr Oumesh Sauba for his powerful software designed to make bookkeeping for your clients easier

50 George Street, Croydon

CR0 1PD

Tel: 0330 056 8705

www.getmyt.com

Oumesh@getmyt.com

BY THE ONE AND ONLY KING CARL MENSAH